CROWD OF SOUNDS

ALSO BY ADAM SOL

Jonah's Promise

CROWD OF SOUNDS

Adam Sol

POEMS

ANANSI

Published in 2003 by
House of Anansi Press Inc.
110 Spadina Avenue, Suite 801
Toronto, ON, M5V 2K4
Tel. 416-363-4343
Fax 416-363-1017
www.anansi.ca

Distributed in Canada by
Publishers Group Canada
250A Carlton Street
Toronto, ON, M5A 2L1
Tel. 416-934-9900
Toll free order numbers:
Tel. 800-663-5714
Fax 800-565-3770

NATIONAL LIBRARY OF CANADA CATALOGUING IN PUBLICATION DATA

Sol, Adam, 1969–
Crowd of sounds / Adam Sol.

Poems.
ISBN 0-88784-688-2

I. Title.

PS8587.O41815C76 2003   C811'.6   C2003-900796-0
PR9199.4.S693C76 2003

Cover: Bill Douglas at The Bang
Typesetting: Brian Panhuyzen

Canada Council   Conseil des Arts
for the Arts   du Canada

*We acknowledge for their financial support of our publishing program
the Canada Council for the Arts, the Ontario Arts Council, and the Government of Canada
through the Book Publishing Industry Development Program (BPIDP).*

Printed and bound in Canada

CROWD OF SOUNDS

Contents

I

A Kind of Singing

*I had the idea that the world's so full of pain
it must sometimes make a kind of singing.*

— Robert Hass, *Sun Under Wood*

THE CALCULUS OF A MAN STRIKING WATER IN RELATION TO A BOAT STRIKING WOOD, AND THE PIECES SHATTERING

Here is where the boat broke through barriers as a hand goes through a screen. How the timbers trembled. And a boy on the bridge whistled like an old man, waveringly. We have seen how the captain used his throat to imitate the ocean. Three girls on the shore were throwing stones at the water, and we wondered whether someone had lost his way watching them. But the boy on the bridge was without guile, and when the boat came through he could only gape, like a window.

The sound of wood breaking is familiar to all of us, even the unborn, but the girls stopped throwing as if their ears had only just opened. And the captain, launched from the deck, made us all think of our drowned fathers, our drowned brothers, our drowned sons. These are things even the boy on the bridge would know by now. In this town there are those who love the drowned, and there are the drowned.

Not even air pushed through the boy's pursed lips could change the shape of the captain's hand as it grasped for the clouds above the water and found only the shreds of the dock.

So we see the boat, the captain, the dock, the boy, the girls, the stones, and the tremblings of the frustrated water, all in relation to each other. And we can use these fixed points to calculate how the boy will return to his mother's home, how he will omit the story of the crash and of the captain thrown from the deck, but how he will repeat the whistled song in reference to the girls throwing stones at the water and the sound of the spray against the falling hand, and the floating wood.

Solve.

WHERE QUIET WORKS

Down where the Indian cemetery reaches its fingers
into the school soccer field,
down past Mohegan Bluffs, near Isaac's Corner,
where the seeds of firs
gather on broken stones,
just far enough from the mopeds on Block Island,
Quiet stretches out the morning.
He gathers the broken arms of the Indians' trees
for firewood and brings them inside,
piling elbows on fingers, sap on scent.
He walks out onto the porch pulling his ear,
and looks for the morning ferry.
When he can see it, he sits on the floor
to draw postcards of the sea —
sparse, the way people like them.
Quiet leaves the cards on the porch under a stone
for the man who comes with butter, milk, and bread.
It is late summer, and the man
leaves a bit more today, a little cheese.
Quiet tends his garden of carrots and cabbage,
eats his dinner on the porch,
reading the birds.
When the last ferry reaches Point Judith,
he walks the empty bike routes,
collects ribbons, a glove, papers, and bottles,
carries them in a woven basket
to a table in the room with the wood.
He fills the bottles with seawater
and rainwater, and taps them with broken shells.

XMAS EVE AT PERKINS

I have strangled the last drops of colour
from an exhausted teabag,
watching a worn-mouthed woman
arrange her deranged father in front
of his poached eggs and tapioca.
He says his first word of the night: *Wait.*
Muzak leaks from flat sieves in the ceiling. No one
is holly or jolly. Short-straw busboys
will us to oblivion in their polyester vests.
A vagrant quietly drinks his tubs of half-and-half,
burns holes in the vinyl seat with someone's
abandoned cigarette. Desolation is a cliché.
Half of what makes him angry
is how he can't escape the after-school-special
episode of his life: here is where
he collapses at the Perkins and longs
for home under a tinsel tree. Are these my people?
Are these my fellow men, their transgressions
tallied on individual receipts?
If I stood in my booth, declared a holiday
of love and forgiveness, and ordered
meringue for everyone, would I be hailed as a saviour?
Or escorted out to the pavement
by the avid manager in his weirdly knotted tie?
Probably neither.
So much for human sympathy.
So much for Joy to the World.
Tomorrow a boy will be born. Even now
his mother strains and sweats. And we're all dreaming
of rest as we reach into our pants and purses
for something to redeem us.

WISHING YOU BETTER

So strange to find you here now,
after our disasters. The snide past provides us
its occasional kick in the teeth.
The whole walk back to your hotel
I've been tracing the scar on my arm.

And here you are, face softened
for ever finer shades of expression.
Your hair has gone brittle since I last
held it in my fingers. You're separated,
and your mother's bottle finally broke her.

Remember the picture at the carnival?
Your face hard as an old lime,
and the sign behind you, daring us to enter?
I dared you to kiss me. I dared you to tell
your husband who you really loved.

It's true I like to think I was right all along,
not just about Michael, so gentle
after he was angry, but about every
stolen phone call, every secret kiss,
every murmur on the soccer field.

Sarah, whichever of my foolish words
still churns inside you,
that is the one I treasure. Even now,
despite the lobby's clank and drone,
when you remove your overcoat,

home wafts from your sweater,
the smell of burning charcoal. I must tell you
that all my hopes from those days
are bees battering windows.
I want to wish you better.

MAN WHO SLEPT BETWEEN BLOWS OF A HAMMER

Was there an immanence, or was it just blank blank blank,
the way white vans might pass through a window's reflection,
sounding out like a brush on a drum? The flick

and flash, and you're going to have to accustom yourself to my
    absence,
as to a broken watch.
It was late, there were rocks in the road,

and I was hiding in the dark dank of the city near the dormitories.
I was in awe of the street cleaners and their terrific appetites.
I was aware of the loneliness of lamps. Then began the mystery,

complete with homemade hats and clever demands.
I was alone, and then grandly accompanied. The young master said,
I don't want your goddamned library card.

It was a festival of denials: there was the No,
and the Nono, and the Please no.

Let's say I never enter heaven.
Let's say my estimable qualities have worn thin as paint.
I could have forgiven if I'd known.

And yet between brutal rhythmic truths
there was plenty of time to remake my remarks.
So what if it was dense with sad-faced boys and their tired
    epithets?

Once, I slept next to an infant prince
and could sense his fear and confusion,
so I invented songs for him in running dreams.

That is to say, I was sorry to be so old.
That is to say, I snored myself awake.
Now, as a runnel of rain fingers through my hair and down my cheek,

and the sense that something has happened passes,
I sing half-syllables through my sleeves.
Another of my failed languages.

PREMONITIONS IN THE VIBRATING SILENCE
OF A DAWN HIGHWAY

Beside you, the shoulder blooms
a violent mosaic of wildflowers.

Summer wind squeals as the car
bursts through it. And there's the faint,

almost imaginary grind of mating
cicadas. If you weren't

speeding home from another
clock-punching all-nighter,

hands swollen, throat dried
up with smoke, this might seem

a pleasant experience. But you
don't even know how bad it is.

There's rust in the exhaust
and the cat escaped while your wife

was leaving you. Still,
you've got fifteen miles of empty

highway, and isn't it a peaceful morning:
thin fog a grey paisley

against the road ahead,
occasional swipe of the wipers

that smears it all into a dirty
streak on the windscreen.

IMPACT

Gracefully the pickup approaches, skating sideways on its axle. Inside is the man who will break our lives in half, like a biscuit. Already he has had time to consider the events his locked brakes have set in motion. We could envy his meditation, or we could wrench the steering wheel, defying physics in our trust of the minivan which had carried us this far without incident.

Our hands have their choices: to incise half-moons into the vinyl armrests; to fumble with the seat belt's metal tooth dangling uselessly over our shoulders; or to reach behind to touch the children, who are oblivious, who understand innately and without concern that we are their protectors.

Have we failed in this endeavour? Will the impact that follows prove that we were negligent in our choice of safety equipment, of route, of velocity? Were we wrong to begin our journey together, when our other car — the more nimble one — crouches grumpily in the garage, its only passenger a neighbour's cat who is batting the antenna and leaving paw prints on the hood? Should we have stayed home and spent the Sunday feasting on tortilla chips and explaining the nuances of the uppercut, the jab?

Apparently. But why pursue these questions when out one side window we can see a mother and her child bundled up against the cold in matching hooded parkas? Isn't that the style we wanted and spent weeks hunting for when the weather first turned? Where did she find them?

PRELUDE AND VARIATIONS

Prelude

He swiped the pistols from the station armoury
and picked her up at the Esso near her house.
It's only when he sees her there, waiting
like she'd done that freezing night in February,
that he knows they're going to do it. He drives
out past the granite quarry, parks where he's
caught high-school kids carousing Friday nights.
He can't look at her until she takes the gun.

Then it's like she fills the car with light.
She puts the barrel in her mouth. "Sweetheart,
are you sure you want to do this? It's not too late."
Yes. It makes her shake to even think it:
to face her husband, Jack, much less the boys.
Better just to end it all with noise.

I

Maybe it was how
his chin sort of buckled
when he put it in.
Or how tightly he squinted.
He wanted to live. And, somehow,
so did she. Couldn't
they just keep on driving?
She had money. How far
was the border? Kansas?
They could get set up.

He counted down his fingers —
3, 2 — why the thumb?
1, and it was over,

and she hadn't done it.
She had even heard
the hammer's small pop:
now her ear was ringing.

He was everywhere:
the windshield, the steering wheel,
the rear-view mirror. Now
she was alone, the rain
a light round of applause
on the roof of the Dart.

II

He'd always known he was a coward.
That's why he joined the force, to confront
his fear. But it hadn't worked.
That was why he needed her.
And why he couldn't handle Jack,
even after the punch that night
at the Johnson's barbecue. And that
was why he waited — just an instant.
She pulled on 1. She'd gone without him,
and burst the crystal of courage she'd grown.

The force of the recoil had knocked
one of her teeth onto the dashboard.
And now, coward that he is,
all he can think about is how
he's going to clean the fucking car.

III

His thumb drops.
There's the taste
of metal, but
besides the rain,

only the roaring
absence of sound.
He turns to her,
looking out.
They're both thinking,
You would have
let me do it?
It ends the way
it began:
with alarm.

IV

FLOOD

1. *3:15 p.m.*

My wife and I sit on Jarman's Hill and watch Saint
Paul working its way south like a wrecked barge.

She thinks there could be children out there,
and we do see a cat, drowned or exhausted,

lying on a miraculous wicker chair.
We laugh. Grab it for the new house, we say.

A lovely wicker chair, cat included, no money down.
She takes a sip from the plastic gallon jug

and passes it to me. It tastes like
the shingles of our house. Shingles

under water, maybe, loyal as a turtle's shell,
or maybe someone south of Saint Louis

is picking through our debris.
If only we knew what was left, she says.

I say, Let's pretend there's nothing left.
Everything will be a gift. I pass the jug

back to her, and she spits some in my face.
We're rolling in the mud on Jarman's Hill.

Where Tim Jarman's gone the river only knows.

2. *11:38 p.m., Shelter*

I'm paring our lives down to the skin,
        what's left.
    Last summer we lay on the bed watching

the curtains breathe in the sun,
the corn full and sweet coming in,
and I wanted to think, Sundays,

but I knew even then it couldn't last. James,
if I lift my chin up to your collar,
lick the unshaved edge next to your ear,
could that save us from all this debris?
Our house has sunk into its foundation,
like a soufflé. Did we

forget something? Some secret
that could have kept ruin away?
Once I saw a glint in the disposal and wanted
to reach in, my fingers
in the half-crushed grapefruit rinds,
but I was afraid of the blades.

I am not willing to give up my hands, not
the smell of your wrist, not one word
you have mumbled in your sleep,
small revisions.
I want to push out into the river, James,
that sinister, random creature —

I want to walk home through the wash
and mud that once was a road.
I want to wade into our yard holding fingers
like we did at the ocean,
back when all our best dreams
had water in them.

HAIL

In Hebrew it's *barad*, said like
      barrage. I should have remembered that from Passover:
"Spill from your cup a bit of wine
      for each of the ten plagues: blood, boils, frogs, hail . . ."

How can you sing
      when my children are drowning? That sort of thing.
And the wine on my finger,
      sinful and sweet. The pictures in our Haggadah

are half cartoon: the printers
      used only red and blue ink. Blue frog, red boils.
As for hail, it took the bus to Tiberias,
      rattling through the Territories like an empty oven pan,

and the stop at Nazareth
      to remind me of the word.
I'd forgotten what hail sounds like,
      how the tongue-rolling of the rain suddenly turns serious.

Story goes the Galilee
      is fertile because it gives back to the Jordan
everything it takes.
      The Dead with its permanent suck. The mostly Arab riders

had gotten off and we were
      ready to go when there was a slap on the roof,
then a click. Stones. The driver whipped
      around with his hand in the travel box,

but it was only hail. Clack to smack
        and the white stones surrounding us as if we were being salted.
We sat there ten full minutes
        while the storm passed over.

Their thighs in the aisle,
        the soldiers and the children exchanged faces.

AT THE QUESTION MARKET

You called me dog, and for these courtesies
I'll lend you thus much moneys.

Don't you think it's time you exchanged that old carcass
for a bag of magic beans?
Here I am, sack full of pretty toys. Look:

thousand-year-old maternity trinkets,
souvenirs from a blood sacrifice,
a bottle half full of light. What pleases you?

Let's not discuss prices until you've decided on something.
I can see your stomach twiddling its intestinal thumbs.
You're wondering what I've got in my pockets,
but there are a few things I just can't trade,
not for a wilderness of monkeys.

Here, instead, make a banjo of this parchment.
Use this skin from my back as a lampshade.
I sell foreskins and hymens by the gross,
and my fillings, well . . . that's real gold.

Consider this wet strip of newsprint
as a replacement for your damaged eye.

SONNET WITH THE MORNING PAPER

We've got grackles stealing morning from the sun,
reluctant, enmeshed in telephone wire.
A raucous tribe, red squirrels conspire
to chatter the neighbourhood from their homes.
Dawn-sensitive streetlights flicker off,
spooking sparrows. Red maple crowded with finches,
starlings, and a crow, Dumpsters and mesh fences.
The bright air — clouds raspy, green, and lost.
A neighbour on his porch whistles "Misty"
over a bossy, grumbling garbage truck.
Hotshot paperboy in his rolling bag of rust
plants a story of the world into our heads:
it is brief, big, and black. Somewhere fifty
students have joined the bloated ranks of the dead.

MR. POLK WAS AFRAID OF THE RAIN

No damage we did to his garden would bring him out of doors
if the slightest drizzle leaked off his rusty roof. After a while,
beheading his tulips got boring so we'd fetch his paper for a
   penny.
He didn't mind us dripping on the carpet.

> *I have been to the meadow,*
> *I have been to the shore,*
> *I have been to the ghetto,*
> *I have been to the war.*

One stormy November weekend my mother tsked
and brought him bread and eggs. He repaid us
with shortbread so buttery it slipped through our fingers.

> *I have seen the boys bite,*
> *I have seen the boys lie,*
> *I have seen the boys fight,*
> *I have seen the boys die.*

Once when I came home whistling
a glory hymn we sang in school, Mr. Polk
beaned me with a half-eaten apple. From twenty yards.

> *I once knew a Thomas,*
> *I once knew two Jacks,*
> *They went out in August,*
> *They came home in sacks.*

When I was old enough to join, I knocked on his door
to show him the uniform. He brought me inside

holding my elbow like he was helping an old
woman cross the street. Showed me
his medals and trophies: two stars, a fistful of ribbons,
and a tooth inside a velvet ringbox.

> *Thomas was hit in the heart,*
> *Jack was hit in the brain,*
> *The other Jack was blown apart,*
> *They all were hit in the rain.*

LETTER BACK

Pluto is fat. He likes to get acquainted
with the new ones before he gives us
free rein of the place.

There are people all around, though,
and they always have a good word for him.

No one here wears ties, or black.
Pluto likes yellow, and sports a great
aquamarine cape when he wants rain.

He told me on one of the first long days
that his favourite diversion
is making up names: Ogaril, Fenerith,

Dunamo. He tries not to fall
into the three-syllable rut, but he knows
what is between him and his beloved
always brings him joy.

I soon saw her, washing her face in the Lethe.
She had a French braid
with dandelions entwined in it.

She said *Welcome*, and later, when Pluto
and Nostradamus were playing Parcheesi,
she took my hand and led me to the Fields
That Are Always Empty, whispering,

I always love the fresh ones best.
The fresh ones remember.

THESE WERE THE DAYS OF BROKEN GARDENS

Mothers overturned their marigolds and jonquils in a collective quest for clues. They ravished their radishes. They broke precious vases for digging tools. Nothing was spared, not even the airtight cases preserving their wedding gowns. They believed if they combed through everything as if for ticks, then one of them would turn up the key, and their boys would return to break bottles and spill popcorn under their couches again. Only a town as perfect as algebra could bring back the boys, the sons and uncles whose majestic hips and dusty shirts had not been seen for three seasons. Where had they gone? Surely one of them would have left a note for a sister to discover. Surely one would turn up at the river with word of a holy salmon run. Instead all they heard were the crickets' needles clicking. No body sounds in the bedrooms. No body smells in the bath. If only they had seen the signs and acted. If only they had asked or answered or burned. But in truth nothing could have stopped the boys from going. They heard the clarion and followed as they always did. Now what was left but to scour the drain plugs and sift the potato peelings for an antidote to that music none of them heard. Sing merry all day all merry. Sing merry all merry all day.

IN FAVOUR

At times I thought he'd rather pull my hair
than kiss me. He was that smart.
Evenings we'd go down by the wade pool

and break the gathering ice with stones —
it was like heaven, only it was brutal.
The vapour from his mouth froze my hair brittle.

People say drowning is the most peaceful way to die,
but I'm in favour of lightning. The trouble is
how to attract it. Joey said I made him sweat,

and I believe that much. You can't keep mouthing
the words to a song without something
escaping from your lungs. But I knew

when I'd broken enough of our wineglasses,
the splinters would find their way under his nails.
He left the kitchen creaking on its hinges, the porch

spattered with gravel confetti. Turns out
nothing could keep me in danger, not even
my love, delicate and fierce as a wasp.

SUBURBAN PASTORAL

Beer can boys in the Grand Union parking lot
throw stones at a No Loitering sign hanging
from a light pole by one rusty screw. Pock. Pock.
Pong. Behind the store, two girls just off work
practise kissing on a pile of pallets.
Another night of beauty and grace.
The local ice cream dive closed down
and the Cineplex is so full of Disney
even the clerks are monochrome. Houses
in the hills are shut tight against the humidity;
infants inside sleep with slight lisps, heads
full of milk dreams. What can we do?
Beats me. Know anyone who needs
to get pounded? Nah. Well keep thinking.
The sign won't give up its post, whatever
they throw at it, even their car's air filter,
so they drive to the 7-Eleven to hump Mortal
Kombat and shoplift M&Ms. No ID
no smokes no matter what you call my mother.
Back at the Union the girls have given up
on the call they were waiting for
and head home to watch romantic videos.
Why can't the boys we know say things like that?
Can't afford the therapy. Next door someone's father
is deciding he should keep a little extra for himself.
Somewhere a shepherd just broke loose from his leash.

THE WEIGHT OF FIRE

Walking down Bloor in March, some sax
playing "Don't It Make My Brown Eyes Blue"
and a bitter rain squinting our eyes. Our shoulders
hunched like pigeons on balconies.
Foggy shop windows obscured the mannequins,
and your skin already translucent from the chemo.
You bought a pack of Kents and we stood
under an awning while you lit up with matches
you'd picked out of the waiting room ashtray.
Your lip curled around the filter, somewhere
between a kiss and a sneer. Now the sax
switching to something sweet: "Satin Doll,"
or "Just the Two of Us." Your knees
buckled under the hot weight of that fire.

SONG FOR THE PATHETIC BUSKER

In the pasty moonlight, this street looks
like a smashed guitar. Wires hang loose
from their sprung pegs
and below, on the road's worn neck, splinters.
Here's the sad-eyed Sunni sleeping on his sausages.
There is Mr. Green calling for an end to colours.
And down by the stairs to the subway, a voice
rages that no one has ever loved me the way
that voice loves me.
An hour ago some drunk kids
overturned his change cap, and the precious
puny fistful is spread about him like trimmings
from his ratty beard. Mostly pennies.
He hasn't the heart to gather them together.
If we were smarter than we are, and more generous,
we might know how to soothe him. He is,
after all, weeping while he sings, if you can
call that singing. But we are all
wrapped up in our own reasons for being out so late.
The last streetcar rumbles past with its hysterical side panel,
and he yawps even louder, like a winged goose.

LETTER TO THE CINCINNATI BILLIARD BOYS

Friends, I am a lonesome tad, it's true.
And it's true I've been seen dragging canvas parcels around the
    neighbourhood.
What's a boy to do?
With everyone chomping their bits to bits,
    and landmen passing off their various grandmothers and caulks,

it's enough to make me crave
even the stink of Eightball's unwashed leather. I'm telling you,
you wouldn't believe the vowels they have up here!
And it's getting so you can't open a window
without letting in a letter. I'm mad with it,
my head rattles like a poor boy's piggy bank,
but I keep my mouth shut for the sake of the saints.

Only you guys know my panic,
and you must promise to swallow this —
            every word, Packy, even your name right here.
If rumours start, there could be no end to freakish
    commiserations.
Imagine me hanging from a door frame
while confused roofers rip out the floorboards.
Send me a good grip.

FISSION

A jay cackles the rumours of summer
and I'm hunched around
the morning in my legs, this brightness.

Now her house: red X's on the wall calendar
counting down to her departure.
I've woken her. She squints

me into focus,
her face close, two eyes becoming one.
Touch the roof of my mouth with wishing.

The words are: *Your sleep is
like water.* Her closed-eyed smile,
canvas of shadows on her winter neck.

I hang my head from the baseboard,
almost to touch her lips
with my dumb lips. Lately the East

is a nowhere between us.
Her pupils contract.
I blur into noises from the street.

BLIND

I can hear the widow upstairs
hallucinating a man
stealing her hair
dry hair thick as weather
but it is only

the son of the Jamaican house nurse
standing on a chair
to change a bulb

I know a student
who is sculpting a shrine of bones
gets them from the meat house
and bleaches them scentless

believe me when I tell you
my street is a frenzy of starlings

if I were heavily curtained
or suspended like a chandelier
I might emit some light

where is there room for colour
in this crowd of sounds
I know as the world

across the alley the redundant
husband plays
a fugue on an uneven upright
with dried-up dampers
and a broken sustain

tell me about your seeing

ORPHEUS IN HELL

                                        Which song?
              Given the magisterial audience, dour

and tone-deaf as the gangster owner
          of a jazz club front for a fence,

given terror and the wet cold which makes
          his fingers feel like chopsticks,

given the ghost of the woman he loves floating
          over his shoulder, her half-

discerned breath behind his ear igniting his desire
          after so much stillness,

given the dark and his flimsy cloak and the fog
          of spirits attending,

where does he summon the nerve to choose
          from the compendia of melodies —

the odes, dirges, chants, reels, and arias innumerable
          wrestling in his mind's ear like worms,

the stirrings of songs unwritten, the samba, ragtime,
          and klezmer only he can predict,

the chorales and laments, banshee wails and saxophone
          groans, Chopin's dying falls, Coltrane's

desperate runs, Ali Khan's ecstatic thralls, Hank Williams's howl,
          Waits's wreckage, Caruso's lilt, and N'Dour's

clear call — all
          he could summon from his fingers and throat

as effortlessly as he could pinch a single note
          from his worn old lyre. But which note?

Which instrument, which timbre, which tone
     and before all the hosts of hell which words?

                              Perhaps
something about how he knows they will
          never reach the surface, how

his loneliness and doubt will betray them:
          a resigned Chet Baker sigh

to acknowledge defeat, a moan from Gasparyan's duduk
          while spirit descends again

into darkness, and a Heifitz trill for the sweetness
          of longing. What else

might convince the Lord of the Locked Gate
          to let Eurydice go but

the mournful promise of her return? And what
          better song to his lover

hovering behind him than the admission
          that his grief is so great

it defeats the very gift which might raise
          her from death?

                    But if so,

then the song we've learned from Apollonius
     and Ovid and Virgil, and

sung ourselves for generations, is it the whole story
        or just the song he sang to Death? A lament

for art's failure or a cover for their escape? No song
        could end with her first new

step on earth, their enraptured embraces,
        and return home to

the blissful drudgery of familial love. No,
        the song must end with his weeping.

II

JOYFUL NOISE

JOYFUL NOISE

1 *Tutti*

> *De la musique avant toute chose,*
> *Et pour cela préfère l'Impair.*
> > — Paul Verlaine

Rumour has it this will be the last Cantors' Concert —
some dispute about allowing a woman to join the committee.

Still tonight, despite the rain and the wires
spidering around the dais under the ark,

we are all together. In the balcony, a Haredi
camera crew videotapes the Reform cantor

opening the show (host's privilege) with his operatic English.
And even the Moroccans seem to enjoy singing

the yidishe lider a bearded redhead
leads from the stage. Believe me, it's no small thing

to see a woman wearing a sheitel in a building with stained glass
windows and a pipe organ. But it's all Jewish music, yes?

Even if the pronunciations are different —
this one sings "sov," this one "tav" —

or even if some of the melodies sound distinctly
Arabic. Look at the cantors during the chorale,

every man's voice climbing on the shoulders of the others,
in sibling rivalry. The Sephardi adds his trills

above the melody, even from his place in back.
And the hazzan from Aish ha Toireh adeptly dodges

the swinging arms of the Conservative conductor
whose kipah is embroidered with a Nike swoosh.

II *Messiah*

> *And Music shall untune the sky!*
> — John Dryden

The program notes chirp: *Join the Maestro's Club for $1,300.*
Not as many Jews on the list as I've seen elsewhere.
Tonight's performance sponsored by Blockbuster.

Rejoice greatly, O daughter of Zion.
Shout, O daughter of Jerusalem.

The soprano can't stop smiling: found Jesus, probably.
Can't say the same for myself, though the bass
is outstanding and the tenor
    is doing his best with what he's got.

A long-haired counter-tenor sings the alto:
Then shall the eyes of the blind be open'd
and the ears of the deaf unstopped.

I'm checking to see which parts are Isaiah,
which parts Luke. Handel's librettist swiped from the Bible
all out of order, and the program notes report

that leading London Puritans scoffed
at such sacred themes being performed
in a common house of entertainment:

"David said, How can we sing the Lord's Song
in a strange Land; but sure he would have thought
it much stranger to have heard it sung in a Playhouse."

He was despisèd, and rejected of men,
a man of sorrows, acquainted with grief.

My Bible at home translates that verse from Isaiah
as *acquainted with disease.*

When they start with the Hallelujah chorus,
my wife says, *We're all Christian soldiers now.*

There's a part of me thinking, Hallel Yah, my God, *mine,*
but I don't hesitate to stand,
and it's not out of some sense of the good faith of humanity,
or the belief in all religions' essential search for truth,

but because of the basses

                     And He shall reign for ever and ever —

because of counterpoint, and the resolution to dominant.

Hallelujahs resolve from perfect fourths, not fifths,
because in the Middle Ages the Church believed
that a five-seven chord contained the Devil's Interval.

Hallelujah, hallelujah.

III *Solo*

Music heard so deeply
That it is not heard at all, but you are the music
While the music lasts.

— T. S. Eliot

Now hush — here's the oldest cantor
to sing his solo.
                    We can hardly see him
behind the clutter of music stands and wires,

and the liver spots on his scalp are glistening.

He's chosen a setting of the Unetaneh Tokef —
a prayer from the Yom Kippur service
said to have been written by Rabbi Amnon from Mainz
while he was being dismembered during the Crusades.

>   *Let us proclaim the sacred power of this day.*
>   *It is awesome and full of dread.*

He later came to a young rabbi in a dream
to dictate what no one had thought to write down at the time.

>   *The great Shofar is sounded,*
>   *and the still, small voice is heard.*

The chord progressions, though, are right out of Beethoven.

>   *The angels, gripped by fear, declare in awe:*
>   *This is the Day of Judgment!*
>   *For even the hosts of heaven are judged,*
>   *as all who dwell on earth stand before You.*

How he gathers himself beneath the notes.
How the fragile body clenches, then releases.
His grandson is up front, his hair spiked green.

> *As the shepherd makes his flock*
> *pass under his staff,*
> *so do You muster and number every soul.*

The other cantors, like boys, poke their heads out
from the wings. They know
he won't be singing like this for much longer.

> *But repentance, prayer, and good deeds*
> *can temper the bitterness of the decree.*

We could shut off the microphones, and the stained glass
windows would still shiver in their earthly frames.

III

HALF AS GOOD AS MUSIC

But I think everyone should have a little philosophy, Thomas said.
It helps, a little. It helps. It is good. It is about half as good as music.

— Donald Barthelme, *The Dead Father*

TAKING DOWN THE SUKKAH

Branches we hung from the roof — roof we could see
stars through — are dry as burnt chicken skin. Leaves

crumble to dust as I begin to hammer down the beams.
Never sturdy, the sukkah fast returns to planks

with protests only from three-inch nails as they give up
their posts. From the kitchen window, my wife watches

red-eyed. She is through with crying, and her mouth
is taut, impregnable. Down come the cards we stapled

to the frame, down the beads and gourds we hung
with lengths of yarn. I carry the damp two-by-fours

to the garage and stand them upright — once again
they enclose only their own space. The cinder blocks

fit neatly into a corner, and the lawn table we set inside,
now stained by rain and raccoon scat, returns to its place

in the basement next to the unopened crib. Done.
Return the hammer to its drawer, the ladder to its hook,

and our lives to a week without dreaming. The last
of our near-child bleeds blackly into the pad between

her thighs. Our festival of flimsy structures is over,
leaving only balled-up tissue, flattened grass on the lawn.

EARRING

All winter she would scowl out the window, muttering,
 It's out there somewhere.

A gift from her grandmother. She lost it running in from
 our first November storm.

The detached garage a raft always drifting farther from its
 square shore. Now,

late March, and the yard finally clear of its residue slush
 and muck, we scan

the lawn like cartoon detectives. The capillary busywork
 of ants, the early daring

sprigs of new green. Overhead a blue jay notes our progress,
 cackling. She runs

her hands through the awakening blades the way she runs
 them through my hair.

Since the miscarriage that's all the touch we can muster.
 My knuckles are still split

from winter's parched air. Two weeks from now I will find it
 wedged in a crack

on the driveway, flattened like a filling. But today, briefly,
 there is this challenge

she has charged us with, and our joint determination
 to locate the unrecoverable.

KITCHEN QUESTION

Once again the cold air clinging. Once again
the chewed pencil, rank sweatpants,

patient roaring of the highway in the valley.
A man sits at a kitchen table amid papers, empty

glass, keys sprayed out like a frozen spark.
The clock with the broken face doing its old work.

He gets up to refill his glass with cider.
All around the house are candy scraps and wrappers

left over from Halloween, which they ate while debating.
I admit, he remembers saying,

we have not exactly lived
up to each others' expectations. It was as if

he had submitted their marriage to a committee
evaluation. That was when she finally

broke the crystal bowl and crashed out of the house.
The slammed door was what the evening was all about.

It's likely she still thinks of that while she strains their Pinto,
blasting the radio, the last of the season's mosquitoes

smashed against the windshield. Or maybe she's already
made it to a sanctuary she'd had in mind for such an emergency.

Now a helicopter from the military base whines
overhead and the fridge responds with a reluctant groan.

How can he question her answer? Wasn't she right to heft
her shoulder bag after all his evasions and petty griefs?

But how to be alone in the house, when even the broken glass in the trash adds its sharp rebuke?

How to get past this to the calmer phase of loneliness? He seems to remember some plan of attack, but now it is lost to him.

VISITATION

Clomped down College singing Ashrei
to the sidewalk. Nurses in sneakers

smoked outside the entrance, recapping
last night's TV drama: *They'll kill him*

so he can make movies. And a cold wind
despite the calendar's insistence, It's May,

May! Maples outside the hospital
still strangle on Christmas lights and wire.

In your room you are biting the breathing
tube. Anything to make something crack.

Then you cough and your face clenches
like a ball of tinfoil. The morphine is wearing off.

Stay still, Papa. Any minute now someone
will come bearing words of truth and light.

SUBJECT: LATEST NEWS

My father's window unit struggles to keep summer
out of his bedroom, but there is still this dampness.
Cars swarm by mourning their lost shine
and cruel mistreatment.
                              I am imagining
a festival of blue jays, and an incandescent key.
There must be a president who knows what I mean.
In all his various lonelinesses, he is enclosed
by those who know him.
I want to bend him over my knee.
I want to teach him a Neapolitan chord,
but it's too late for levity. He's gone.
Already the man in the white fedora
is sweeping the street with the vicious precision
of a spider.
                    I knew a man
who could balance a table on his chest
and even he has collapsed from want of certainties.
And my colleagues preaching Revelation
have only a few months' wait to be wrong again.
However long the day, someone will recap it.

Meanwhile my father's heart debates
whether it will brave another squeeze.

ON JAYS

Songs are poor, mostly raucous.
      — Birds of North America

There's a story of a dozen jays dive-bombing a cat
to keep it from a fallen chick. And the one about a cat
who hunted down a dozen jays. Scraps of blue
strewn about the lawn like a broken balloon.
I heard that one at a party while trying to eat roasted garlic cloves
with someone who resembled the Grinch. I miss those parties.
There is always plasticware left over.

There are countless tales of jays chasing sparrows and chickadees,
even squirrels, from feeders. There should be a study
of the various creatures who thrive near humans. Enough
of these *National Geographic* specials on the snow leopard,
the California condor, the humpback whale. I'd like to see
a one-hour program on pigeons, or mosquitoes.

Mammals of the New York Sewer System!
Birds of Suburbia: wrens, grackles, and jays. Turns out swans
don't always mate for life. We could learn
something from these programs about what it takes
to live with people. For instance, all these animals are cruel.

Crows, chipmunks, gulls. And of course the roach,
Crown Prince of the Urban Habitat. Roaches would be much less
repulsive if we couldn't hear them walking.
I once said that roaches only want to live together peacefully,
but I'm not so sure now that I've spent more time in New York.
I think roaches are waiting, like you wait at the house
of a sick uncle whose piano you'd like.

Jays eat roaches. When it has one, it looks like the jay
might just be transferring it to a roomier apartment, it holds
the creature so carefully in its beak, and the roach moves its legs

with what could be wonder.
Tickles the tongue, all that horror in the mouth.
Then a quick flick of the head, like swallowing a pill,
and it's just the jay lifting its feet, crooning a raucous jazz.

STUNT

                    In the film,
you are shot through the head
by a man wearing suspenders.
He is not all bad, but for you
he is bad enough. After that,
they tow you out of camera range
and you are free to die again,
perhaps as one of the extras
wearing masks. As it turns out,
today the industry is feeling
generous. It's exciting to imagine.
With everything so crooked, the unions
and such, it must be reassuring
to die, perfectly, your cheque
as good as cashed, your left hand
raised in supplication
(in honour of the esteemed
tradition), your trademark gritted
teeth, eyes glazed,
expertly portraying the agony
and fascination everyone
in the audience for one moment
shares with you.
If you are lucky, you will have
the opportunity to die four
times in the coming week:
as the villain's officer,
an innocent bystander, a helmeted
policeman, a form thrown
from an exploding building.
Meanwhile, behind the wide
pan camera is a hack who's just
learned that his liver is tumorous.
Go to him now and show him how it's done.

BLUES MY DADDY TAUGHT ME

Blues for Tommy Two-step
Blues for Einstein's Brain
Blues with No Mint Julep
Blues, I Missed My Plane

Cold Blues in a Snowdrift
Blues in Central Park
Blues for Moral Uplift
Blues Afraid of the Dark

I Left My Blues in Pittsburgh
I Can't Get This Blues Right
Blues for Eddie Ginsberg
Whose Mamma Died Last Night

Blues for the Orangutan
Blues with Bloody Feet
My Uncle Was a Bluesman
Your Blues I'd Like to Meet

Blues That Fixed My Rifle
Blues in an Apple Core
Yeah, Sing This Blues My Wife
Will Kick Me to the Floor

Blues That Shines My Shoes
Blues for a Telethon
My Daddy Taught Me All My Blues
Blues, Where's My Daddy Gone?

YOU SAY

it's marmalade I made you out of plums
skin fruit and juice you say goddamn would you
shut up you talk so much then you say baby
c'mere you say I'm sorry you say hush

you say I know that you've been screwing around
you say clean up this kitchen for once you say
turn off that TV you say lover like
the word is on your teeth and you can taste it

you say words that don't have spellings words
no one can hear you say where'd that money go
you twitch your foot when you fall asleep your head
is on my chest my hair against your cheek

your hair is creeping up my neck and your mouth
is open I can hear that slow breath rise
it isn't what your words mean that I love
it's what you say so slow it takes all night

MONK HUMMING

If I were deaf I'd pay ten bucks to see old
man Rudy's jowls sway to the beat, his eyebrows
so high on his face he appears to be in a constant state
of amused surprise, as if he'd expected nobody to come —
not tonight, with snow packing the streets
and the sidewalk a treacherous
scramble through frozen footprints
always smaller than your own.
Here we are, though, elbows propped
on the sticky tables crowding Rudy's piano
so that if the woman in the green scarf
spilled her drink it would soak his dampers,
and a geek in front with a pocket video camera
keeps bumping the trumpet's mic stand.
And lucky for me, I'm not deaf. I'm even sitting
close enough to get below the music, the easy beat
and lazy vocals Rudy sticks in between solos.
Amid snaps of the snare I can hear
the intermittent sound of him humming.
Maybe it's the song he sings for himself
while he bird-walks the keys for the rest of the room.
You can hear the same thing on Monk's records:
his voice breaks into "Well You Needn't,"
no matter how the hapless sound editor
cleans the masters. Suddenly there's the man there
behind the alien chords and falls — the rattle
in his chest, the lazy tone,
breathing through his forgotten nose.
Jimmy Rushing's wife shouts from the sound room
in the background of "Bright Lights, Big City,"
and before Manse Lipscomb starts on "Meet Me at the Bottom,"
there's the sound of him licking his lips.
These are the broken eggshells of the music.
At the bistro tonight, I am listening in
on an old man's private monologue —
off-key, forty years younger, and smoking.

THE ORGANIST

The madman asks to hear the song again.
She smiles, and looks around for someone else
to rescue her from his insistent question.

He interrupts their churchly celebration.
The congregation, disturbed, grooms itself
while the madman asks to hear the song again.

They're confident someone will help their friend
while she, recoiling from his damp smell,
seeks rescue from his now repeated question.

It doesn't come. The lonely, patient madman
makes as if to join her at her bench,
asking, "Could you play that one again?"

At last the madman's son appears, resplendent
in Sunday best, sporting a snakeskin belt,
to rescue us all from his father's question.

He leads the man away, returns to mention
he has recently purchased an antique barcarole.
He'd love to hear her play that song again.
Who'll rescue her from *his* insistent question?

THE OBOIST

As she aged her perfect
     pitch bent
flat, so that even her oboe's
     clear nasal tone
maddened her with insult.
     All those years
making her closed lips sing
     and now her own voice
rang shrill. She was fired
     from the orchestra
for playing the *Ode to Joy* in B.
     "The way your wife's
face looked after her stroke,
     that's what my music
sounds like now."
     She tried to rewire
her stereo to play
     her records at 28 rpm,
but in the end she just
     sold everything she loved.
Now she loiters in the train yard
     listening to the engines
changing tracks, the screech
     and crash of the metal,
and she thinks, "Dying C-sharp,
     ascending A-flat."
She is always wrong, but
     when was right perfect?

THE PERCUSSIONIST

Mostly I stand behind the kettles, counting.
    I master

the subtle changes that make a boom
    a crash.

And I wait for Copland's *Fanfare*
    or Ravel's arrangement

of *Pictures at an Exhibition* when
    for a moment

I play melody with my blocks, bars, and skins.
    No breath, just touch,

but everything I play begins to fade
    as soon as it is struck.

If it is the dream of every woodwind
    to strike something with force

then it is mine to sing a woeful note
    and hold.

HOLDING ON FOR DEAR LIFE IN LUMSDEN, SK

I've been singing my tick and beetle songs
incessantly to the hills, but still there is

rejoicing. Boys bounce on the roof,
and swifts are scanning the mustard for moths.

You've heard the old adage: phenomenology
is a spectator sport. And anyone can see the leopard

frogs are in no hurry to escape your gaze.
A kingbird committee is discussing our troubles

in the limbs of a dead ash, but the results are as yet
indeterminate. Perhaps there's a serving of smoked

meat that may help us resolve their questions,
or a screwy cue to bank us home. At any rate,

there are cicadas and reasons to be something less
than desperate. Listen how the tractor in the valley

snuffles as it goes about its work. Hear the sneezing
cleaner in his luminescent cloud of liberated dust.

Oh, it's true, there's a fine line between leisure
and terror, but meantime let's mash the turnips

while we may, and sprinkle sugar over our doubts
and derelictions. I can see the moon

careening over the horizon with murder on its mind,
but it's still a long way off. Minutes, at least.

DEATH BY SOMBRERO

If Cherie hadn't slipped
and punctured the child's arm with her knitting needle
if the cow had not crashed through the fence
which kept it from the water
brown water choked with lilies
if the king had ordered his troops
to Pull back! Pull back!
if anyone had stepped on the button
if the carburettor had blown on the tractor
which whirled and ground plants into dust
that blew into his nose Carly
would not have removed the hat
would not
would not have wiped his brow
with his dark forearm shining with sweat
would not have spat into the air
would not have sneezed
would not have shaken
would not have fingered the circular scar
would not have seen the end of the world
would have instead
clasped his shoulders with his opposite hands
and called to the hills Yes
I see what you make of it

MRS. MOORE'S BRIDGE

About a half-mile down the road
from my house — you'll find it if you get lost —
there's a covered bridge
stretching to cross a stream. The sign
on top of the arch sports artwork
by a local woodcutter. "It's been standing well

over three hundred years," Mrs. Moore says. Well,
that's what she says. You'll see yourself the road
is too flat to be old. Construction workers
sealed soda cans into the supports, and even the lost
stream has cement chips and rust in it — sure signs
of recent construction above. And the bridge

itself is built like no country farmer would build a bridge.
But it suits Mrs. Moore just as well
as any colonial thing, freckled with signs
left by musket balls that missed. No road
around here has generated history since they lost
Danbury to the British. No harm her working

a bit of half-truth into her story, the light work
of it making her face younger as it bridges
the space to her past. Let her be lost
in a memory she can't place elsewhere. "How well
that bridge stood up over the road
when the storm in '41 carried the sign

on the old firehouse — remember that sign
my Billy and his school friends worked? —
clear over the reservoir to Barnum Road.
As a matter of fact, that's the same bridge
where Henry first kissed me. There's a well
there we used to visit. Feels like a week since I lost

him." Mrs. Moore talks a lot about loss,
how the world used to have a design
she can't quite read anymore. "You may as well
forget about me," she says, the patchwork
lines on her hands wrung dry. "No one knows that bridge
like I do. You only know the road."

THE CONDUCTOR

With all the power rushing past,
amazing that he doesn't fall.
We stare at his galloping back,
his sharp gestures an angry teacher's.
No wonder we get a little nervous.
On the platform he seems small,
whipping his baton so it curves,
a peacock feather.

Arrayed against him, musicians in black
rub horsehair on catgut, burst their lungs
forcing air through tubes, or strike
surfaces of assorted tensions
with what can only be called relish.
I worry that if the man does one thing wrong —
instead of French horns, asks for English —
the whole fiction

will explode: mass fermata, winds
discarding chewed spit-swollen reeds,
oboes flung at violins
they've always resented, trombones at last
up front, carousing, brutally loud . . .
I almost want them to succeed,
but he restrains them, saves the crowd.
Brahms advances

in stately fashion, as he deserves.
And though there's plenty to see, for once
our eyes are not our first concern.
The players, tamed, grumble in pairs,
but obey the conductor's stern commands
like good grandchildren. They become
an orchestra in his sculpting hands.
They trill the air.

SONGS WITHOUT WORDS

She sat up today, ate soup.
Her wrists are blue as the nightgown
she would twirl in when
we still spoke with our mouths.
Later, I'll change her sheets,

hearing the "Spinning Song." The last
piano I heard playing it
had a tinny C-sharp.
Sometimes she catches me
weeping at the window. If she can,

she smiles. She floats in and out
like the left hand of a "Venetian Boat Song."
When she's asleep, I go downstairs
and sit at the piano bench.
I don't want to wake her, so I hover

over the keys. My fingers trace chords —
Confidence, Regret, Consolation —
romantic pieces of our old life.
Every few hours, I go upstairs
to put ointment on her bedsores.

Deaf as I am, with my hand
on her back, bony as a fish,
I can feel when she groans.
I'm humming Mendelssohn.
It helps her to sleep.

TORNADO WARNING

The basement window bends with the strain.
Siren's started again.
Eight miles away at forty miles an hour,
our past twists back to name us.

The radio gurgles warnings: *Cover
your head.* So I lift you over
me again. And with the comforter downstairs,
we are safe. We spin.

When the rain starts in earnest,
we are on the floor, the farthest
we can get from the sky.

The wet, our breath — beads
on both sides of the glass. It's here. We
deserve this weather.

GROUP IDENTITY DATA CARD

Please check the appropriate boxes. Are you stallion, mare, or colt? Have you broken any article of the Mosaic Code? Yes. No. Not sure. Are there holes at the bottoms of your shoes, literally or figuratively? Has your brother beaten you for daring to drive his Big Wheel? Have you repaid him in grief? If you have not instructed your children concerning the manner in which you would prefer to be buried upon your death, what will be the process they use to determine it? Analysis of your wishes. Analysis of their wishes. Analysis of expenses. Other. Do any of these solutions strike you as callous or cynical? Do you believe you have a contract with God? Account for your paper usage over the last three weeks. Below is a list of categories which may or may not refer to you: Indigent. Salacious. Melancholy. Homosexual. Vietnam-era veteran. Watchmaker. Orphan. None of the above. All of the above. Not sure. In the space remaining, please state your purpose.

JULY 4

On my drive home, soundless
　　　bursts of light like failed stars — not even
the permanence of an airplane's roving flash.
　　　The moon blushes orange for the occasion
before turning in early with a quiet excuse.

My neighbours have stuck small flags
　　　into the ground near their mailboxes,
as if the posts were soldiers' tombstones.
　　　I think I'd like a mailbox for a tombstone —
instead of balancing stones, my family
　　　could leave letters some groundsman

could burn. Arthur Ashe, dead for years,
　　　spoke on the television today about condoms
and charity. Now the pops and whistles
　　　of liberty. It's the earth readjusting itself
to summer, the shift of vertebrae. Everything
　　　feels edgy, on the verge

of some quiet collapse. Frogs' and crickets' steady
　　　groan, the occasional boom.
My life, the skin of a balloon.

ACKNOWLEDGEMENTS

The following magazines and anthologies have published these poems, some in earlier versions. Many thanks to the editors:

Amethyst Review: "Death by Sombrero"; "On Jays"
Antigonish Review: "Holding on for Dear Life in Lumsden, SK"
Chattahoochee Review: "Where Quiet Works" (as "Tacitus")
Crab Orchard Review: "Joyful Noise" (as "Sacred Music")
dig: "At the Question Market"; "You Say"
Event: "Subject: Latest News"
Flying Island: "Song for the Pathetic Busker"
Grain: "The Calculus of a Man Striking Water in Relation to a Boat Striking Wood, and the Pieces Shattering"
Louisville Review: "Stunt"
Malahat Review: "These were the days of broken gardens"
New Delta Review: "Tornado Warning"
Portland Review: "Songs Without Words"
Response: "Hail"
Southern Poetry Review: "July 4"
Texas Review: "In Favour"
Wind: "The Weight of Fire"

"Blues My Daddy Taught Me" was published in *Why I Sing the Blues*, edited by Jan Zwicky and Brad Cran (Vancouver: Smoking Lung Press, 2001).

"The Weight of Fire" was published in *The I.V. Lounge Reader*, edited by Paul Vermeersch (Toronto: Insomniac Press, 2001).

Thanks also to the Canada Council for the Arts.

I am deeply grateful to my friends, readers, and editors, who lent all sorts of help and encouragement, especially Al Moritz, Ken Babstock, Vivé Griffith, Michael Redhill, Don McKay, and the Colloquistas of the Sage Hill Writing Experience. Most thanks to Yael, for her faith, patience, and love.